Poems and Prints

John William Holway

An Englishman in Exile in Hamburg

December 2018

Bibliografische Information der Deutschen Nationalbibliothek:
Die Deutsche Nationalbibliothek verzeichnet diese Publikation
in der Deutschen Nationalbibliografie; detaillierte bibliografische
Daten sind im Internet über dnb.dnb.de abrufbar.

© 2018 John Holway

Herstellung und Verlag: BoD – Books on Demand, Norderstedt

ISBN 978-3-7528-1540-5

Contents

Music

I often play music to lighten my soul.
I wriggle my body, to move is my goal.

The blood in my veins needs to flow, you
see. I need to move, to let go and be free.

The words of the song speak so clearly to
me. A message of hope to take me,
where I long to be.

Some songs are angelic, while others
quite rude, the music vibrates my body,
and lifts my mood.

I dance to the music I feel the beat. To
the magic of the song I move my feet.

My body pulsates, my energy rises, music
you see is full of surprises!

A special Person

At the end of the day, take time to begin, to focus on the light that shines deep within.

For in each of you dwells a bright shining star, just remember how really special you are.

You have so many talents and so much to give, just be quietly thankful for each day that you live.

Take time to listen and time to be still, do good to others and never wish them ill.

When you're feeling lost, alone or forlorn. Remember what you do makes a difference, that's why you were born!

Be kind to others, treat them as they should you and always take pride in the things that you do.

When you're feeling angry, frustrated or sad, think of the good times, don't dwell on the bad.

Remember the "magic moments" and outbursts of joy, when you let yourself go as a young girl or boy.

When you share a feeling - your joy will increase, and remember that the stars never cease....

to shine so brightly in the sky far away to remind us all where we're heading one day..... So at the end of the day as the night draws in

take time to listen to the voice deep within. Raise your head up high, look above your inner wall...

for learning to love yourself .... is the greatest love of all!

Early in the morning

Early in the morning is a good time to pray. I can tap on my keys as I swing into the day.

Early in the morning I am at peace, for a while my worries and cares can cease.

No one disturbs or wants something from me. I can be at my keyboard and feel so free.

No one to get cross, or tell me what to do. At last I am free, and can think of you.

I thank you God for being here with me. You are so precious, so dear you see.

You know how I feel, you know what's up in my heart.

With your grace each day, I can make a new start.

From you I can't hide, from you I can't run, you know my needs and with you I can have fun!

For you are God you never leave me, you know how I am, and how I can be.

You are God and you bring Heaven to Earth. This is the miracle to which Jesus gave birth.

After we struggled and endured the long night. He came to those in the dark, to bring us the light.

He came to give hope, to give us life everlasting. His love is for free and there for the asking..

So open your heart and let God's love fill you.

With Him at your side what can you not do?

Happiness

Happiness is now. Happiness is here.

I feel the light. I have nothing to fear.

**I am totally present. I am fully awake.
There is nowhere to go. Nothing to do, or
to make.**

**I dwell in the present. Not the future or
past. This world you see, is often going
too fast.**

**Folks often dwell on yesterdays and
things of the past. They cling to
memories, which can never last.**

**Or they fret over the future and what
might be.**

**They are fleeing the moment; they are
not present you see.**

It's time to bring spirit, back to your body. Breathe in breathe out and sit a while with me.

Enjoy the moment and savor your life. Give thanks for your kids, your partner or wife.

Be grateful for your body, FOR you are unique. You have all you need. You need no more seek.

You are so precious, each one of you.

Do all with love, whatever you do. Today is your chance to come *home* at last.

Don't rush to the future or dwell on the past. Just sit and relax, maybe laugh or smile.

It's good just to sit and BE YOU for a while.

Denglish

I become a beefsteak, my girlfriend say to me.

She be blonde and beautiful, she not thick you see.

I be live in Deutschland and I say you to you.

We kenn us very good

We meet us in the zoo.

I speak with you auf English

And yes you must cum with.

And see my Stadt named Hamburg

Zis is who I liv.

I am loving very much the English, but please think me not rude.

I find it hard to eat the soggy English food.

The chips are cold and crunch not, not sharp enuff for me.

Za beer is flat not frothy, there is no head you see.

I would the Queen Elizabeth, much very like to meet.

To kost the fish and chip and to go on the Baker Street.

The English love their weather and never do complain.

They always wear umbrella, because it often rain.

They are so kind and polite, even policemen smile at you.

And most of all I like it, that they say "Du" to you!

GOT TO G0 GO

I've got to do the dishes. I've got to make the tea.

I've got to ring my mum, and be back home by three.

I've got to read the paper and get some letters done.

And if I don't get on I'll be in bed at one.

I've got to change the hinges

on the garden gate.

The squeak annoys the postman

it really cannot wait.

I've got to watch the telly

and read the Evening Post.

I've got to iron my shirt,

don't know which I hate the most.

I've got to ring my auntie, to make a date for tea.

We're booked up every night, I hope she isn't free.

So many things I've got to do

so much still to be done.

It seems a daily battle

which never can be won!

You won't find God

You won't find God if you're moving too fast. Your life will soon be over, a thing of the past.

You won't find God if you're rushing and dashing about. Your mind full of worries, of troubles and doubt.

You won't find God if you're always on the go. Always on the move and never going slow.

It's hard to find God, when you're always in stress. Your inbox is bulging and you're life's in a mess.

You won't find God if you always want to speak. He comes to the lowly, the mild and the meek.

If you want to find God, take time to be with Him, and with yourself you must begin.

Let God into your head and into your heart. Allow Him access to your every part.

Speak to the Lord and start to pray. Find time to listen, for a while each day.

Find time to be still, to be silent and just to meditate. Hush your busy head and then just wait.

If you want to find God, I know where to look. Just open the Bible and read in His book.

Let Him speak to you softly, for He loves you very dear. If you look for God He is always near.

See Him in the flowers, in the bright sunshine. He made all the creatures and reigns divine.

Feel him in the wind and the fall of the rain. For after the storm, the sun will shine again.

See him in the faces of people you greet. Many an angel may be found on the street.

Hear Him in the laughter of those whom you love and daily give thanks to the Lord above.

If you want to find God, He will find you.

So just slow down and let Him,

show you a different view.

Amen

Hope

There are some days in your life when you just can't cope.

But take heart my friend, there's always hope.

Hope is the magic that makes a man merry and gay. I wish you hope for just one more day.

Stay in the moment, just live one day at a time.

Don't drown your sorrows in whisky and wine.

Don't waste your life doing drugs and stress.

Your body will become an awful mess.

Focus your thoughts on nice people and places.

Look at the smiles upon their faces.

Hope will help you change perspective in life.

Let go of worry, of trouble and strife.

Release your grumblings and cast your care.

Accept that life is not always fair!

With a stock of smiles it's easier to cope, a friend is on hand to give you hope!

"No Time"   for Christmas!

I've got no time for Christmas, now "laß mich bloß in Ruh"! (leave me in peace)

There's only 10 days left and still too much to do!

There are so many presents, which I still have to get

And all those crazy "shoving" shoppers, which really make me fret!

There are so many things which still just must be done,

Christmas is so commercial, it really is no fun.

I've still got to buy presents for auntie Ann and Fred,

Why don't we just abandon Christmas & spend the day in bed!

And Grandma needs new knickers and Grandad a new vest. I never know what size to get, it really is a pest!

Those Poke Moany thingies which all the kids have got,

If I found the Jap' inventor I think I'd have him shot!

I've got to bake the "cookies" and the tree must be "geschmückt" (decorated)

All this work preparing, makes me quite "verrückt"! (crazy)

So many Christmas cards, which I still have to send.

Uncle Bert and auntie Gill - the list seems to have no end!

All those Christmas trimmings and that silly Santa stuff

Folks just never know when they've had enough!

And the office parties – all those G & Ts, It makes a stout man weak, and tremble at the knees.

I've got no time for Christmas, I REALLY am "gestresst"

I think I have forgotten, the meaning of the "Weihnachtsfest"! (Christmas)

So for once this Christmas, remember DO make time,

This really is the meaning of my little ryhme.

So do make time at Christmas for peace
love and good will.
Spend some time with loved ones and
make time to be still.

Remember the true meaning of the
"Weihnachtsfest!"

Be kind and love your neighbour, & be
good to all the rest!